Life in the Blind Spot

Life in the Blind Spot

Poems by Raymond Barfield

David Robert Books

With all best wishes —

Raymond Barfield

© 2013 by Raymond Barfield

Published by David Robert Books
P.O. Box 541106
Cincinnati, OH 45254-1106

ISBN: 9781625490551
LCCN: 2013952468

Poetry Editor: Kevin Walzer
Business Editor: Lori Jareo

Visit us on the web at www.davidrobertbooks.com

Acknowledgments

A number of these poems have been published previously in journals including *The Midwest Quarterly*, *Free Lunch*, *Timber Creek Review*, *The Carolina Quarterly*, *The Florida Review*, *Fulcrum* and *Slant*.

For Don and Molly Verene

Table of Contents

I

Looking for a, Thinking of a.................................. 1
Salt Bones and Holy Sands.................................... 3
Geography and a Thumb....................................... 7
Driving.. 8
 Chronicles of Iddo the Seer............................. 10
A World in Multiples of Two............................ 16
The Koan of Close-to-Death............................. 17
On Formally Undecidable Propositions........... 19
Saint Augustine by the Sea............................... 20
The Singing Tree... 22
A Ruin in Fog.. 23
Doll in a Porcelain Cave.................................... 24
Man Rejoicing on Hot White Sand.................. 29
Winter Boughs.. 30
Fruit Basket in a South Carolina Trailer Park.. 31
The Dog of Pompeii... 34
Grackle on the Wrought Iron Fence................ 36
Life in the Blind Spot – a Love Poem.............. 37

II

A Mystery for Breakfast.................................... 41
Bishop Berkeley's Sermon................................ 42
A Slight Haunting... 45
One Evening I Took My Mind for a Walk....... 47
Brown's Serenity... 49
Crow on Telephone Wire Just Before a
     Thunderstorm... 51
The Playing Fields In Winter........................... 52
At the Window Drinking Tea........................... 53
Girl in the Doctor's Library.............................. 54
White Itself... 55
The Labor of Waiting....................................... 56
Librarian of Passions, Cooking Dinner............ 57

Staples on the Telephone Pole............................ 58
Stonehenge and the Impenetrable..................... 59
The Bridge of Sighs.. 60

III

Putting on a Face.. 63
The Blues Player on Beale Street....................... 64
Mosaic in the Gutter... 65
Quill... 66
The Surgeon in the Evening after
    Demonstrating Certain Controversial
        Techniques.. 67
Illumination Hides the Stars............................... 68
Santa in the Ginkgo Tree.................................... 69
Archimedes of the Five and Dime..................... 70
Autopsy on Christmas Eve, Without Refrain...71
The Blackbird Breathes the Ghosts of Night...73

IV

An Introduction to Memory in Texas and
    Beyond... 77

I

Looking for a, Thinking of a

When the pelican glides
along the surface of the sea
with a motion of the wings as smooth
as the calm morning
ripples

and my own slow rise from sleep
it does not think of flying
unless some unexpected thing —
a wave, or a stone out of nowhere —
topples it,
the flying more a stand
from which the clean horizon is searched,
movement, yes,
but supporting another aim,
the finding of a fish to eat
as the eye looks here and there,
the motion very nearly adjusting itself.

When the pelican glides
along the surface of the sea
searching for the elusive fish,
feeling with biological symmetry
that the flying requires the catching of the fish
and the catching of the fish requires the flying,
it topples me
and I am suddenly aware
of my mind gliding along a rarer air
utterly mind-like
in its unmindfulness
searching up out of sleep

and suddenly swooping in
on the pelican swooping in,
what we do to survive,
a fish here and there,
or the clean sight of a single pure thing
answering a pleasant hunger
on lean days.

Salt Bones and Holy Sands

I

From sand blown into curves by a night wind
the morning smelts cold sheets of black
layer by layer, condensing yellow to silver.

A white air burns the serpent's eye.
If Leviathan had rotted on the shore
his spine might glint like sharp barbed wire.

The lizard zips along the dry hills, stops,
runs, breathes, thrusts his tongue, the blood
red tongue that splits a small and holy air

gliding from the borders of Lebanon with cedars
to the hills of Israel where avocados grow.
The tongue tastes residues of nomadic ghosts:

Moses on the cliff, and Christ in airs;
Mohammed with his raised pen dipped in ink
the color of the scuttling lizard's eye.

II

The dead sea needs no grave the desert sand
cannot provide. In moonlight the sea shines
like a medallion on the desert's breast.

This may be the only war the desert
ever won against the sea. The sand
forever cradles the defeated corpse.

The sky and clouds may swallow parts like vultures
leaving the glistening, white pillars of salt –
the bones of the sea's hidden skeleton.

But the desert wears its victory well,
far from the cares of any living thing,
a salt and battle older than any claim.

As to the scattered men from so-called wars
these are dismantled by the quiet tongues of dunes,
or left to shade the lizard in his thoughts.

III

Under rocks where Christ's foot may have passed
casting familiar shades of man-sized shadows
the spiders hide from sandaled passers by.

What mists the God incarnate may have breathed
as spirit rose to clouds and moistened wings
by providence became the silver rain

that wets the laughing heads at street cafes
now giddy from the burst of noontime wine.
They feel their skins are much too small for souls.

What sounds of warriors' feet, what deaths of lions
accomplished by the shepherd's stone and sling
reside as memory on Israel's hills?

But still the stretched smiles that bare the teeth
and hiss the strokes of vengeance to the clouds
reveal the truth that meanings fix our grief.

IV

The ruins of Rome are ribs around the old
Jerusalem; and calm Golgotha's skull
stares at Zion's heart with hollow eyes.

The stones along the paths no longer seem
the kind that might erupt in mouths and sing
hosannas in the shadows of the palms.

On streets the merchants' nostrils flare with cunning,
breathing air that mingles with the sky
that spreads across the towns carrying dust

from land to land. There is no place to hide
from sacred recollections. And the soul
can only guess at where the lizard goes

who slips through chinks in cobbled streets, descending
past where water fell from Pilate's hands
down to all the patient dead, down to roots of stone.

Geography and a Thumb

The geography of my grandfather's mind retains
the shadows of forgotten thunderstorms.
Its foundation is a temporary scaffolding.

Scattered in these dry lands
are feelings with a calculus
of stones and strides and other man-sized measures.

When he translates that crumbling world
into a tale, his finger rubs against
his thumb, coaxing from the depths of flesh

geography marked with boulders
set at crossways of invisible paths,
and headstones, and millstones.

He needs
no new experience to fill
the wandering. Brown on yellow hands

he rubs as if the history
of love and pain resided
in the tip of that crooked little finger.

The tale is never finished, he rubs to say,
pulling up the grave array
of the farm boy's aches. He's words
and earth. The path up. The path down.

Driving

From Memphis to Mississippi
potholes loosen faint ideas
and the time between ideas.

Girls along the road with that old
perfection, that vacuum
of beauty drive the beast.

Love the girls in Fords jarred
by cracks contracted in the dry
winter with no sweetness in its breath.

Love the girls that bud each spring
from behind the most surprising trees
with grins clenched along the fence

rattling among mufflers stiff
with power, shaking in youth,
rusting, rotting in the humid years.

Dogs beneath the telephone lines
flash eyes of fear and fearsome
loyalties, legion among cold stones.

The rhythm of the potholes,
billboards, gravestones and local police
grown up with advances in irrigation,

girls new to their periodic lives
and transience add up like every tale
to the singular longevity of the whole.

They saunter to the billiard hall
where members of the local bestiary
press chance in the swamp

of cigarette smoke, residues
from bottles of beer,
and the marrow of a greasy rib

so the lips glimmer in a sly smile
calculated to guarantee resiliency
of home, a veritable world.

Chronicles of Iddo the Seer

Wound

Who would not be grateful for a running sore
to distract from the vague ache of unuttered
loves? As a boy he tore his knee
tripping over the worn pick of a master
mason. A girl – not quite a woman – tended him
as his new-rumbling heart drew healing heat
through the wound while she pulled the rag
from her head across his knee and held it fast.
The bleeding stopped, or else there was no blood.
Blood collected in the static depth of his heart.
The winter wound bled white.
Now an old man honored by dishonor
he safely picks his teeth and watches the world,
still limping from emptiness.

Vision

From inside the coffin truck the world
seems less in need of trinkets than before,
less inclined to notice seasons change,
and given more to shadows of memories
that raid the mind like fishers wading depths
angling past the pates of struggling spawn,
the starts of flesh and culture's murky base.
Vessels hold the shades of dread in sheets
as all that now is atmosphere of home
submits to fears of neighbors and to calm.
Iddo sits inside the sliding door
with the merchants counting out their change.
The world's commercial meaning warms their days,
the calming calculus of just returns.
From inside the coffin truck the world
is parsed up into wager, price and yield.
A way to name. A way to understand.
They discount coffins bought in twos or threes.
The tremor in their cries disguises moods.
No matter what the politics or faith
might say of crisis, victory or defeat
the merchant knows the lift of gratitude.
And never bothered by unanswerables
a certain price is placed on all relief.
Though commerce sees an optimistic world
they dust the coffins, faces tuned to grief.

Gift

The world is not a virgin, nor ever was.
The spider dances on the sticky web
quilted with providence.
The rabbit and the rattlesnake share
dunes blown up by ocean winds.
All night the tree frogs scream their passion.
Insects waste and die.
The world is not a virgin, nor ever was,
and Iddo is at home among the thinning webs
and songs of wet obedience.
Seed of tree and honey bee upbraid
his own peculiar goal of chastity.
In solitude he endures the weight
that skirts the lip of emptiness.
The world seems, and seeming, all comes down
to this: sight, a true and subtle gift.

Rest

Iddo finds a place inside decaying
trucks with loosened hoods. And insects find
a home on rusted cams where flowers grow.
The global satellites might pass above
the sleeping man in the deepest part
of night with hums like Aristotle's stars.
He thinks the messages of time and war
reflected off the tumbling crystal balls
must hum, omniscient monitors of the world,
as he picks at rust and vinyl cracks
upon the dash. The ground is visible
beneath the rusted floorboard while above
the rusted roof reveals the light of time
and tiny dots of light that move along
to gather secrets from the universe
and from the governments of enemies.
But Iddo's eyes see meaning in the stars
and meaning in the eyes that look at screens
with blips of light and signals of a kind.
He feels it as he feels his weeping knee:
he knows no satellite can reach the stars;
but what resides in mind can feel the far.

Love

A boy with one eye sat near Iddo's plate
and drank clouded ouzo from his cup.
Strings of tawdry decorations hung
along the walls, cobwebs of festival.
The boy was back from the colored lands
where he wandered and had his skin tattooed
with winter, fall, and the bloom of the flowering seasons.
He spoke of secrets from the tombs where winds
whisper their way through twists and pains of love.
He said the memory of love is where love tends,
and drank with the confidence of the dead
mumbling about thoughts unwritable in his flesh.
Iddo felt a father in the stranger,
felt his unborn sons and daughters stare.
He bowed and thanked the nameless boy who looked
upon the world with the dry clay eye of love.

Time

Iddo's gift is an excess of sight.
He reclines in his sinking boat
sopping white tears from his wounded knee,
aware of the balance of breaths
that still feels
filled with consequence.

There is more in the world,
a certain feeling of night,
of the way her hair
fell across her eyes as she
went to cure the wound, and wounded
him deeper still.

So many ways,
so little time.
To fill, and feel
and smile
even as the water of time
trickles in and the boat lowers with the sun
and the water of time rises
and so little
breath
and so much time

A World in Multiples of Two

The shadow of the dying man of ideas
passes unnoticed by boys on the sand.
He watches them make a world of order
with a ball and boundaries made of sea and land

as he sometimes sees the shadows of the birds
without seeing the birds overhead, ideas
passing over and through his mind.
Some he thinks, some he merely feels.

The boys navigate with an inner sense
enthusiastic binaries of play
while the man of ideas passes by
the panting beasts a world away.

The Koan of Close-to-Death

To sip the wine of an aging mind,

a wine so clean and given,

to sip the wine of memory

like a cool fermented girlhood
that found its way
through an ungirlish maze
and now dictates to scribes
the axioms of divine grace,

the wine as clear

as the silence of a foreign peasant
        beside the road in dust
        writing brush in hand
        thinking inscrutable thoughts
        and smoking a well-rolled cigarette –

to sip

ignoring the glass

not thinking
how much or how little is in the glass,

and sneaking up on the question

when?
catching the answer

unaware

    perhaps napping in a backroom
    the door just slightly open

On Formally Undecidable Propositions

When geometry
shows up like a traveler
looking for a conference of ideas jostled
in a smoky bar among amorphous shapes,
let jewels snuck from the jewelry box
be a preening child unmindful of what she holds.

Let there be something so irresistible
about uncertainty in a clean world
that even if virtually confined to the system P,
it must finally end up
with the sweet smell of homicide
and the restless detective with his chewing gum and badge.

There will always be undecidable propositions:
a sheaf of papyrus with tantalizing fragments,
a folktale ending with the teller's grinning silence,
the feeling that comes to an otherwise cool mind
when it trips across a child's bedtime story
of Bedouin tents smelling of dates and camel hair.

All that can be done
is to extend a sincere and speedy apology.
But facts are facts:
every day somebody uses a screwdriver as a hammer,
and tables and chairs are propped up by books.
So, great mathematical conclusions are pulled
to the work of metaphor
like well-educated foreigners mopping floors.

Saint Augustine by the Sea

With time in mind old Saint Augustine
felt the grit of God's puzzling ways
irritate his soul, like sand in his shoes.

Turning toward a sauntering shade he said:
friend, come hear my song, fry some fish,
feel an ancient leisure and count the stars.

I am no puzzle solver. I pretend
no sobs; I pull my nets, though I despise
no struggling worm or beast, no not the least.

When lights of dying skies' epistles rage
a shining epitaph against the night
luminous in a lover's sky-kissed eyes;

when all is shaded by the drives of beasts
or fears of gravestones' stark finality,
then I shall silence mouths and speak no lines.

No, I would not seduce the world, but learn
to let the world love me with flaming darts
and all the curves of lust and marks of greed.

Though souls be worn by lapping waves of sin,
on shores of sea-ground skeletons I've loved.
I wade into that sea and back again.

I recollect a joyfulness from youth;
I did not notice age was slouching in,
listening for what melodious groans erupt

beneath the weight of ardent rues and fires
of wordless memory. A true regret
must be the task of youth, not billowing age.

Today the morning sky looked more like dusk,
looked more like skies from tiredest ends of days.
How long I've lived on fish and memories.

By slate-gray oceans' blank and mumbling hums
I do not pick my wounds: I am too old,
too old to learn that all the worlds and lands

are grains of sand and grains of sand and grains . . .
I keep some hope, some gratitude and then
I wade into the sea and back again.

I've had to plan my work on days where death
and miracles both stay. Yes, I have seen.
I've touched disfigured knots on sinless trees.

And though the fish and bread have fed the blood,
eternity cannot disrupt my death.
What is left but sleep? I rest my head.

The Singing Tree

Inside the magnolia
a choir warmed up
passing around a note,
a musical hot potato
new-age alien.

Beside me a local bum
stopped to listen too,
head cocked, intent
as though the orchestration
revealed, and finally revealed,

the meaning of birds.
Lifted out of myself,
barely a peep among peeps,
I said, "Lovely." He said,
"That's why I'm standing here."

When the backfire of a truck
scattered the hum
I left the man waving his arms
while the tree grew
squeaky crazy.

A Ruin in Fog

Three stones stacked,
once a threshold, stand alone
like the smile of the Cheshire cat.

Entrance,
the noun and the verb blur
where fog is involved.

Three roman stones
still inviting,
now to something even older.

Doll in a Porcelain Cave

I

Running from the familiar
bamboo following
her father's fear.

In her hands a porcelain vase
a well-shaped emptiness.

II

He is an ancient man
lodged between lime roots.

Folded up and pale
the lithe Chinese
heavy in his thoughts
chews on grass.

He raised the girl on ideas
like meals of leaves.
Now she achieves revenge
by silencing the bird
locked in the cage of her chest.

Her inscrutable silence might be childhood,
or the numbness of mute fear.
But he suspects the flavor of war
as she lashes out in play.

III

Reposed in the venerable vessel of age
he is occupied with the hairs upon his chin
and he is still
with the stillness of not
answering the grave
glances of the serious girl.

IV

How can eyes so young
be so open
staring at history
made permanent
in recent kilns.

V

The way a fierceness
is made more fierce
by the calmness of the foe's eyes.

VI

The white vase
with its perfect idea of white
beneath a cracked glaze.

Images flash up the side
like flame on the wall of the cave.

It keeps the shape
of the white lime hill

grown up from centuries
of tortuous drips.

VII

The infinite vase of her eye
glazed with water
holds the world
holds the sea
as certainly
as the sky
or the cup
of dead perfumed leaves.

VIII

A small world
an escape into smallness
pressed until the smallness
is nothing,
utterly incapable of imperfection.
IX

The tall grass of memory
grumbling beneath the Gingko tree
waving its paper flags;

trying to find beauty
in the sound of munching leaves
or the way the stem rolls upon the lips.

X

The sky at the mouth of the cave
is more like flame
than ever
revealing its unconcern
in refusing to consume.

XI

If there is terror
in the dust
it settles
in the dripping cave.

This wet sadness
comes from the thought
not of death
but of death's relief.

XII

She makes a world
of pebbles,
a family of dry leaves
formal in their stiffness
some as veined as the elder wise
some blushed with the color of the young
made to walk
with a slight twisting of the stem
by the benevolent child
not inclined just now
to feel the crunch of leaves
in the small warm palm.

XIII

The China girl
squats by a stream
of her own making.

No power can force the truth
of the girl
intent upon a perfect world
bringing forth stone gardens
from the accidents of lime

finding the very way
things ought to be.

Man Rejoicing on Hot White Sand

On the feminine dune
that makes the nomad thrill
a solitary man,
a tree of nerves
distillable in clear liqueurs,
beholds the life given him
and knows joy.

Sand carpets roll toward blue water
beneath the wild, unlikely fronds
where a few sticky spider eggs
bloom in the dryness.
The buzz of a bee
becomes a substance rough and real.
From the white sand he lifts a lizard
traveling away from bounty.

In the desert without fear
of untreatable maladies of mind
he holds the lizard
and watches the eyelids
retract in wariness
at half the universe suspended above,
and he is
calmly amused
like a stranger watching the town parade
or a prisoner
chuckling at a memory from childhood.

Winter Boughs

Winter is no place
to catechize the bird
among the needles of the pines
and haunts of winds.

Its languages are suited
to trembling jaws, its short crisp words
speakable in grunts through beards
heavy with a crust of breath.

The perfect eye
inside the patch of brown on white
peeping with a heart of ice
accuses us

of borrowing winter for our minds,
Advents of ice,
Lents of clear skies
holding on until

an Easter of pollen
grins up from the dark
asking nothing of the sky
beyond the bees,

and sprouts in a warm spring of worms
swimming the shallows of the earth,
the season of wounds bubbling green
through the clean scape of winter's skin.

Fruit Basket in a South Carolina Trailer Park

Whole worlds reside in the worry
piercing the wind-rattled boundaries
of her corrugated trailer tin.

Clusters of lean pine trees sway
casting shadows through dusty windows
darkening the worn arms of the recliner.

In the kitchenette
on the brown, folding table
is a sun-ruined watermelon. Waste.

Nothing but distraction caused that melon
to rot in the back of the station wagon
through hot days and nights of pale fluorescence.

She'd say there are worlds in the wooden dryness
of the seeds like prayers, like monks
swimming the cool cathedral air.

But that melon will go to the bog
of the compost pile with other moon-fed rinds,
and kids will bash it open. Waste, waste, waste.

Her fierce eyes appear at the window,
staring into the window of the next trailer
where a mother peels oranges,

tip to the basket of fruit by the watermelon,
then fall questioningly on an avocado.
An apple a day. There aren't any apples.

In a sack beneath the sink
are peach pits, hard and wrinkled
like old chins.

Seeds she understands, solace in winter time
when the trees are abstracted from their leaves
and the world is no longer blurred by so much fruit

and flesh. The winter clarifies.
The skin grows closer to the bone.
She has seen it, she has seen the same:

icicles like teeth bared on the barnyard door;
the quietest quiet of animal quiet
hanging like a drape on the house of slaughter;

the bodies of the new spring's laughter
paddling among the lilies,
placidly writhing in the fishing pond.

She understood the unseen green and hungry parts.
The ferocious pond was always calm on top
with silent, violent fish below.

That child once saw the world's everything.
But wisdom had to wait for a failing heart preserved
in a tin trailer. With a bunch of wasted fruit.

Now she holds the truth –
how you ought to live this life,
and how to cook with Charleston spice.

The Dog of Pompeii

The day before Vesuvius turned inside out
the always believable dog sniffed around
the market with its mix of salt and fish.

He waved his slightly pulsing nose in the air
for something beyond the smell of sex and work
at the borders of the baths, something beyond

the smell of weeds and urine behind the stage
where the actor was almost emptied of himself,
having distilled a reign to the motion of a hand.

The dog's wet nose drew a chaotic shape
noted by the thinker meditating upon his porch
glad for Pompeii, glad to ponder the dog

bowing his head to sniff beneath the window
of a woman, hands above her head, arms
like an ogee arch, mounted upon her husband.

On that final day of worrying for the man
accidentally dousing the dog with a libation
guarding his fate against what killed his father

the change in the air was too subtle
for the dog to unravel, so he returned to his master,
a fat happy man celebrating his wealth.

Let's drink to the future. But the dog knew doom
beneath his paws. Why is your tail between
your legs? Why is your bowl still full?

Grackle on the Wrought Iron Fence

Something feels finished, done,
something in the cobweb-colored smoke
scrambling from the chimney,
in the way the kudzu clings, digging its fingers deep.
Tufts of uncut grass hang through the gate
loitering in a time of scarcity.
No more enchanted pies of four and twenty
cool on the cracked window sill.

Meanwhile the luminescent grackle, known in stories
for wingtip flutters and a caw like a rusty hinge,
merely eyes peeling flecks of sweet lead paint
for his own nest of twigs and discarded fluff,
as winter is a practical thing
and something is always straining to begin.

Life in the Blind Spot – a Love Poem

I suppose by now it is a well-known fact
that despite the apparent continuity
of what is right before our faces
each eye has a blind spot.

There might be an entire universe, I have heard,
which is exactly the same size
moving with Leibnizian precision
in concert with my blind spot.

All sorts of things happen there
hinted at by children's fables,
by several mythic gropings that suspect
more than the world to be the case.

I sometimes flick my eyes very fast
back and forth to see if this universe
or even one corner of it
will flash into the seeing eye

and then back like it's attached to a spring.
It never does, as perfectly coordinated
with my blind spot as Santa Claus
on Christmas eve. If it peeked out, who knows

what studies might be funded to explore it
perhaps with questionnaires passed around
among the citizens of that universe
to be filled out with a number 2 pencil.

Better that it stay in the blind spot

allowing wonder. I would like to spend some time
saved up from the leftovers
of days that went by too quickly

and stretch a hammock across your blind spot.
I would lay in it with a glass of wine
feeling the breeze as the circle of that world
moved about with your busy glances.

I would watch your face in my leisure
as you go about buying extra cookies for the kids,
thinking of what we all will wear this week,
stopping, looking in the mirror a long time.

Of course, eventually it would become too much
and I would want to step out
and surprise you, give you a kiss.
That is the uncertainty of life in the blind spot —

uncertain whether you can step out
once you are in it, or whether it is like staring down
from Heaven, wishing for reunion,
with mixed feelings about what that implies.

II

A Mystery for Breakfast

In the new snow
the footprints go
only away from the house.

Snow is a trove unto itself,
a white brain
waiting for the impress of memory.

The footprints go only
away from the house
raising many questions.

Bishop Berkeley's Sermon

You cricket; you crocodile;
you tale of earth in Africa,
you gypsy traveler over Spain;

oh you my dying trout,
you fox frozen beneath the snow
skirting dark infinities of hope;

all who swallow unpeeled lemons of sunshine
and drink in the red moonlight at harvest:
Good morning my little congregation.

Do not fear, I'll alter nothing – you shall see
the horse is in the stable and the books
are in the study as before.

If my Sunday notes on onion paper
say that there is nothing in your mind
beyond ideas that feel like things,

I yet embrace the bulging belly
of the bright young girl
who shall be glittering in old age

recollecting wiles of the budding child.
You 'possum on the high fence post
panicked in the child's lantern light,

no place to play dead –
there is room for you too
and all manner of escape,

I give you back the world.
Reach out and feel the very thing.
Oh, wallow in the pond

where brown foam laces the stiff
waterweed at attention,
head tufted by some yellow fluff.

Keep also the crab clicking his meaty hands
impatient with the forward-moving world
and rightly distracted, and to the left.

Pay no mind when I say
a fluxion is a ratio of evanescent increments,
for I have said nothing

almost exactly, a witching good phrase
populating the world of vigorous conversation
with the ghosts of departed quantities.

Keep your colors, keep your wild
nights of joy and pain,
your dreams of quiet faces –

though they leave you trembling.
I am giddy, friends, with the inexplicable
joy that haunts my thoughts of death.

How I want to drink the sky,
to kiss the swollen womb.
Drink my ruddy clear-eyed child.

Nothing is lost here but the weight;
nothing is lost and therefore
nothing, in purest wonder, will be found.

A Slight Haunting

Elephants
along the circumference of the circus ring
look for an exit at the proper time
as children eye the empty swing
high above the safety net
threatening a history of
close calls, of
what if the net broke, of
what if it was too narrow;

the art of slight hauntings,
those absences as subtle as the sibilant s,
lending sentences their hiss,
those, for lack of a better word, things
constituted precisely by their lack
of presence – a universe might be populated
with such faint streaks as disappear.

Some lullabies are fixed in culture
and so less vulnerable
to the demise common to childhood
memories, like the elephants
from the whole history of circuses.
These are the lilacs of evening thought

(from Arabic *lilak*, from
middle Persian *nilak*,
from *nil*, indigo –

not the *nil* that is
the contraction of *nihil*,
Latin for 'nothing' –

no, the *nil* from Sanskrit
nili, from *nila*, dark blue)

finally uncovering
as they move into darkness
whole worlds in the night sky
(once thought of as the heavens)
that we might never know
except for the long gift of light,
this massless grace of stars
dusted across the quiet survivor's eyes.

One Evening I Took My Mind for a Walk

Often I do not have time
to allow it to sniff out all the places
it finds interesting,
all the places where others
recently passed.

But this night I had some leisure
so we went walking
and I followed behind watching it
scurry around curious objects on the ground,
wandering up to clouds to sniff out their shapes,
approaching a woman across the street
so that I had to pull it back quickly
before it lingered and got me in trouble.

Usually I can see
why it is interested in passing over a thing –
a grate in the road stuffed with pine needles after a rain,
a window filled with yellow light
in a house with one old car,
or, again, the lovely woman
passing on the other side of the street.

But sometimes I can't see why a thing so grabs its attention.
Tonight, for example, there was a lamppost we've passed
on nearly every recent walk we've taken.
True, the dusk was settling
with that ominous density
that precedes a thunderstorm.
And I cannot deny that the wind
seemed to rouse itself

with an unexpected vigor
causing me to press my hat on my head.

I would even go so far as to admit
that the swirl of leaves around the lamppost
was rather sustained, not to say magical,
and the shadows cast by the chaos of leaves
wound around the lamp like snakes on a caduceus.
All of this, of course, is a wild stretch,
when the question is why
after the swirling settled down
it wanted to sniff a while longer.

Undistracted by the bones of my similes and metaphors
that I held out to lure it home before the storm,
it seemed more interested
in prancing around the base of the lamp
looking up the oxidized surface to golden light
as though something marvelous
had passed a short time before
endowing the lamppost as a thing
with a mysterious residuum
that I could not begin to understand,
though for the sake of my mind, I was willing to wait.

Brown's Serenity

The numb bliss of anonymous skulls
propped just so upon the shelf
leaning as though intently aware

of some elemental music
delighted Brown in his stuffed chair,
feet crossed and bare on the ottoman.

Around him were cabinets of butterflies;
soft memories of dusted color
fanned out from dry and business-like centers;

all the Amazon and Africa
condensed in velvet boxes, a kind
of meaning to what was once his mind.

How still he is. And all he meant
to do when as a child he saw
the eyes retracted in the skull

and knew that he had seen a truth
within the mummy unexplained
but tarried with in philosophic style.

His chair is velvet; and his vest
is buttoned with the coins of gold
he found on one Egyptian dig.

His nails are quietly reaching out
from hands and feet, cold and pale.
The radio plays Brahms and Bach.

High above, the oily lamps
that once framed Brown's serenity
no longer give the aureate beams.

Crow on Telephone Wire Just Before a Thunderstorm

The old man smoking on his porch
watches the bird bob up and down,
a black cork over staggering, unseen depths,
riding the telephone wire,
turning its head
now toward the first white crack in the sky,
now toward the old man.
He just nods and winks at the bird
as one kept from fear
by his small grandchildren clinging
for joy to his safe, sore knees.

The Playing Fields In Winter

Whatever it is that holds down the dead
grass and bends the limb over the meandering boy
slips between foot steps and the treeless tongue

of a leaf cracking a death
rattle, just as a thousand more buck and
clamor unshielded, corralled by wind,

a chorus, consonantal,
in loosely knotted lament
suited to ordinary time.

At the Window Drinking Tea

He watches the sea's horizon stitched with birds
that rise and fall, a sinusoidal sweep
above the men in white boats who drag
knotted nets along the sea's dark floor
lifting whole cities of shrimp and fish
while the lighthouse warns of nothing new,
low light arcing where shores lie
and surface rhythms of the clawing waves
conceal by seeming not to seem at all,
broken forms thrown to shore, a blunt
retort he takes to say how much of care
is foam upon material crests that pound
to make of salty souls and water's calm
indifference the music of a psalm.

Girl in the Doctor's Library

She curls up, keeps out winter
with a quilt from her grandmother's youth
and reads old books bound in hides.
Sometimes a creak from the attic above
reminds of the large and ghostly mouth
lolling and licking its gothic lips
preparing for a calculated scream.
She crawls back into a bookish silence
where nature's ways are brought to light
while memories tucked in the cedar chest
choke on flannel of a homely weave.

White Itself

Some days I'd trade a whole museum
of toilets, cubes and panels of white
for one afternoon of idealized form.

I'd take four of anything –
apostles, seasons, ages of men
or some other cosmic quartet

laying out the world thus and so.
And having achieved an eternal balance
I'd take a touch of female presence,

though it is true that the draped hip
often draws the crazy-eyed demon
peeking around marble pillars

from the fringes of the lit world and in time
some renegade disciple paints only the fringe
until sense is undone and we ask again

for the perfect execution of white itself,
a safe profundity free of the wild sublime
like church after a bad drunk.

The Labor of Waiting

She lives life now as a snapshot
everything precisely in its place,
an old habit of cleanliness.
Though there is little movement in
her room, she is not at rest,
but alert to the very order
that is her room, and thus
to the most minute intrusion of disorder,
 so that when death comes
she shall be lifted out of the room
as a jewel is lifted
from a perfect ring,
the prongs of her rocking chair
setting forth then and for a time
a perfect, polished, ordered emptiness.

Librarian of Passions, Cooking Dinner

Alone in her socks
she waits for dinner to rise
up from several of the dead
things found in her kitchen
one winter's night. She loves
death spiced and crumbed,
fried, roasted, smoked
and washed down with wine
in her peculiar solitude
lived among discordant refrains
from the corpus of burnt flesh,
martyrs, witches and the like
whose stories resolve upon
the browning of a bird's skin.

Staples on the Telephone Pole

Pockmarks, bare bones of memory,
really no more than simple *thats* –
that a dog was missing, that
my art is on display, that
you too can lose weight.
Near the reverie of staples
where each *that* disappears
in some rivulet of history,
an old woman stares at me
from the crevice of her shawls and raincoat
dragging her bags close to her feet
not quite ready for that.

Stonehenge and the Impenetrable

The stones, huddled like girls
whispering secrets in the halls,
organize the universe
around mystery, layered and unsolvable,
as do girls huddled in halls
like the stones arranged like girls.

The Bridge of Sighs

En route to prison
the eyes turn from feet
tucked in shabby shoes
shuffling along the stone
to the last vis-à-vis
as the world grows smaller
and yields contemplation
of abstract clues
in patterns of cracks,
stones read over years
like holy documents,
the grammarians of crevices
acquainting themselves
with histories of grief,
the seizing of ideas,
a fictional prism of what if,
and horizons made
of nothing more than thought
hurled from windows
and plans mislaid.

III

Putting on a Face

With full trust that the captain
was sure to get the plane down
safely, the old Lebanese
woman who had distracted me
from my reading with her crunching,
her irritable bossing of the steward
and her crinkling of empty peanut packs
reminded me of real desire
during the descent
as she put on her lipstick
and touched her neck with sweet perfume
like my aunt used to wear,
getting ready to meet the man
who would be completely unannoyed
by the charming way she nibbled crackers,
amused by the crumbs on her blouse.

The Blues Player on Beale Street

Set back in corridors of flesh
his eyes open to tree branches
breaking up the light he reads,
hieroglyphic, daily news.
His bones fit among roots, his mind
climbs a green lattice of ideas.
He wipes the dew from his hair, then God
and he make a formal quiet.
When the rhythm of creatures wakes him fully
he rises in search of those reservoirs
of memory hidden in crypts, alcoves
and fonts of baptismal water, a bottomless
well of error and poetry
until he arrives in the alley of blues
and sits beside the girdled whore.
Her eyes full of hunger irk him,
jewels on a dusty grail,
pools of weariness, pus and age.
He takes his pen-shaped clarinet
and dips it in the dark well of strangers
passing by, his improvisation
a block of ice in a hot world.

Mosaic in the Gutter

The rule is difficult to discern,
but as the boy rummages through fragments
of design, something separates
this cube of colored glass from that,
a steel shard, a plastic polygon.
Yet something fine about that world appeals,
where things resemble and are like, a world
that is a world of reminders and hints
scattered in the dust of wrecked windows,
taillights, mirrors and other worn and broken
forms of clarity and illumination.

Quill

A language gin
effective where most diminished,
the point made
where the point was made,
an instrument of intent
dipped in tint
with whole worlds
running down the bony parts
of wings, hooks
in the seas of abstraction.

The Surgeon in the Evening after Demonstrating Certain Controversial Techniques

After the inverted world
where inner things are outer things
and bellies unzip
full of trumpets and domes
the surgeon's eyes close
under the helmet of his skull,
Mozart fills the room,
and he sits with the beast
who occupies his house
sleeping in the day,
but at night alert
lying beneath the hanging hand
cracked from washing.

Illumination Hides the Stars

Some require a heaven of forms; some
need nothing more than the chaos of night
and ancient dread gnawing on a pen.
Both eventually look up and see the past
push its way through a daughter's face
preening, unmindful of mortality.
The formula seems to be desiring seek,
seeking find, finding love, and loving
learn to hate whatever separates.
But sometimes this is not enough, and so
the secret of heaven was leaked to give back
a worn humanity, to keep from breaking hearts.

Santa in the Ginkgo Tree

The music in the house is holiday generic,
the decorations composites of green and berries.
You can hold the manger scene in the palm of your hand.
The season has apparently forced a temporary
lull in several local hostilities,
as though we are going to have Christmas dinner
at least one time in peace, dammit.
But the scotch is nice. And the light snow outside
reminds me of something or other from childhood.
And indeed, across the yard is the Ginkgo tree
lit and turning white in the night, strange
for having a stuffed Santa doll draped
limply in the lower branches. The red suit
is frayed and the white ball on the cap is gone
after several seasons of hanging there,
a quiet joke among small battles,
a family trying to remember certain things
at Christmas illuminated by light from the swimming pool.

Archimedes of the Five and Dime

Something calls from sand and shells
worn by oscillating waves.
Inside his room the hourglass
measures the fluid turn of days.
When Archimedes stocks the shelves
he whistles tunes his mother sang.
She kept the meter with her foot
while snipping off his childish bangs.

"Understand what underlies
the world to be among the wise."
So his toothless mother said
while she stroked his father's head.
Archimedes of the Five and Dime
seems to have a gift for time.

Autopsy on Christmas Eve, Without Refrain

The flesh finally revealed as the great thief.
The boy, head tilted back as though
swimming toward the surface of the pond
foot caught on a root. We begin with the question

"What child is this?"

thinking of a triptych by Bosch, panels open,
the middle one a garden of delights, a challenge
to paradise. Or panels of the advent calendar.

Organ by organ the recital reminds of Frankin-
sense gold and myrrh en route to the manger
on camel backs roughened by hair and the firm
juts of horny vertebrae, the ribbed
box of the manger like a ship with a cargo
smelling faintly of animal nestled in
the calm lowing, before
the slaughter of innocents.

What question is illuminated
in all this light making the reds redder
and the yellows more yellow?

A star, a star, shining in the night,
a fact and the meaning of the fact,
as the heart is like a poinsettia leaf,

or as Francis Bacon, taken with
"Pope Innocent X" by Diego Velazquez,
painted "Head Surrounded by Sides of Beef".

Head surrounded by sides of beef.

On Christmas eve. Silent. Holy.

The Blackbird Breathes the Ghosts of Night

Beneath its belly the rotting bridge
shades the spider and the water bug
alike, their worlds separate
above the flow of melted snow.

A vineyard makes a nest for memory.
The local roots and ivy spiral
like hair tangled in a comb
of broken trellises and posts. Eyes

watch where slack-jawed history treads
with a heavy step to common time
in four by four, like dance, or else
like measurements of wooden boxes.

Stillness. In the winter air
the cat curls on the frozen stove
as dinner scratches in the walls.
The sky above is blue.

The leather tongue of leaves
is moist and lies upon the porch.
The rest is quiet,
home to emptiness.

Stars brush the mounds
feeling for buried promises.
The deepening darkness breeds
the quiet beyond quiet.

It is the birds

who turn to luminescence
of the eyes, listening for rattles
in the throats,

a final song, then rise on wings
and find themselves
waving in the tops of trees.
The matted world is hard to leave.

IV

An Introduction to Memory in Texas and Beyond

I

Dark and clear. Dark and clear.
Whole myths breach the seas of thought
as skies suffer the silver stars
that traveled over Mexico
and by the hand of Providence
now light the wondrous fires of mind
within Divine Camillo's head.

He is alone but carried by
economies of swallowing mind
contrasting with well-wrapped wives by fires,
or with the tea from samovars
warmed to delight the alien breast.

He drives his Eldorado through
the dust of sunbaked Texan planes
following a faded map with lines
of longitude and latitude.
He likes the broad expanse of night
more than the certainty of dividing light,
and sees in all particulars
the promise of universal thought.

Though his girth is far too wide
for health, he fits his mass and thinks
lean thoughts beneath his hunting cap.

The world for him is metaphor
enlivening shades and husks of flesh
surrounding the invisible.
He does not speak of concrete facts
but lolls through generalities
that turn the wheels of memory
like water passing by the mill
or ether propagating waves.

II

When he bends to change his tire
glad for ordinary things,
a certain busyness comforts him.
He is known to nod and wave.

But all the while beneath his cap
he feels the winds of wonder blow.
The start of thought depends upon
the planets hovering in the mind,
the impenetrable blue of day removed.
Camillo feels the night sky's song
that floated past the pyramids
and shook the gates of border guards.

When he drives on asphalt roads
trusting that the road continues,
hoping that no turtle crosses
underneath the speeding wheel,
hoping that no crack or flood
undoes the work of roadway crews
or disturbs his country's petroleum veins,
he knows the calm of his well-fed brain
is bred on more ancient topographies.

Should his massive body lean
too quickly and his spirit fly
a more eternal memory
shall thicken for his phantom eyes.

III

The Eldorado's radio
hums a sheet of gray-white static,
a curtain around his motionless mind.

The theater of memory is dark for now.

Where the black sky meets the plane,
where the heavens touch the earth
eludes the stricter measurements.
There familiar infinities
are lurking in the finite world
reminding of creation's banquet of light
into which meanings playfully retreat
stilling the wan philosopher's pen.

His eyes drift to the rear-view mirror
and he lets his thoughts drop farther back
to feel original axioms
on which material truth is built.
The watery mirage is the static of light,
and all his thought is a gray flat plane,
a sea with barely a ripple from wind.

Deep beneath the surface swims
a whale, the whale who swallowed the truth.
He waits. He summons. He conjures. He waits.
The lure of any speculation,
which is the lure of memory,
rests partly in the noble lie.

The theater of memory is dark for now.

IV

Through all these dunes of gray dawns
neon at the low end of the highway,
a sign, a bauble of significance
to mark a pilgrim's start or harbor.
The diner is a cave of clean blue light
where waitresses shuffle with plates of eggs,
and blink, and nod, and calculate
the bills on pads of greasy paper.
The truckers move in an ancient pattern
and know the meanings of here and there.

Camillo feels a solitude
though all the elements to grow a world
recline upon the vinyl booths
and carry plates in crooks of arms.
He wants to eat his meal before
the waves of the sun's monotonous light
cap the sky and close the world,
disturbing the clean expanse of black
where over the border questions are cast,
anchored in starts and roots of thought.

The reunion of divinely parted halves
nearly makes Camillo swoon
as simple things quotidian
always rest on a layer of night.

V

So Camillo submits his flesh to breakfast
and presses his toast to the egg's sunny side.
O, how the sun craves darkness
lighting all that is given humanity
to do naturally and without art.

Memory is awakened over all that is made,
the work given to a sandaled humanity
bringing forth from the womb and earth
all that strikes the heart to song.
He has walked over monstrous dams
made with the palette of nature's laws;
the way they raise the mortal cranes
high above the mountain peaks,
their art of time and its measurement,
their art of air and of martial games
are kin to their urge for reluctant gods.
He thinks, what a miracle is a man.

Forgotten things remain yet human
to the patient and ordered eye of mind.
Sacred things shall mark the place
where the earth does more than satisfy need
and becomes a pillar of thought and prayer –
the negative art of a stillness not death.

VI

His Eldorado speeds along,
a gallery enclosed in glass.
He sings a lusty aria
conducting with his fleshy hands,
observing how they flail and point,
then makes a speech of means and ends.

Every speech Camillo makes
is of the inside and of the outside.
A ruler can measure the height and width
of the foreheads of marbled kings and saints.
Flesh, he asserts, is the acciaccatura
of all that world of form and thought.

The memory of flesh is limited,
susceptible to accidents
of variation – now protruding,
now diminished by weight loss programs
or statistical waves of famine and heat.
What are the parts of Camillo's flesh?
Brain? Breast? Loin? Flank?
And more in no necessary order?
He sees these parts in butchers' shops
and is aware of man as a cause
and of the folly of a headless nature
organizing flesh and blood.

Yet he can think of the form of the form
of a form of a form of a form of a form,
and as his mind thins into silence
he can feel a twitch, or smell his coffee

and know that mystery and the truth of the whole
encompass even the late news show
where prior to reporting some tragic fact
the reporter makes certain his hair is combed back.

VII

The morning meal noisily digests
making the sounds of borborygmus,
requiring not a single thought.
To ask why his hands have brownish spots,
to ask how his bones articulate
is to speak to elements of a world not his.

His depths repose as sheen or song.
The world he sees is inside out.
He spies out meaning in the spark of a face
knowing nothing of glands or ducts.
A requiem mass occupies no space
unlike the corpse which is nothing but mass.

Yet Camillo chuckles at finitude
as he drives to the west on the Texan plains.
Above, the cloud in the shape of a whale
floats on airs determined by law
as Camillo's digestion is determined by law.

His mind relentlessly squeezes out
some transient beauty from their passing shadows.
Beauty dances on the steps of law.
The retreating phantom of watery mirage
that is one illusion brought by day
is remedy for none of that curious thirst,
which is the pain of memory's heart,
which is the joy of memory's art.
The foundation of beauty cannot be deduced,
nor the fire of secrets in the unmeasurable part.

VIII

In the eyes of another he sees the world
distant and anonymous
turn and stretch toward his mind.
These secrets straddle day and night.

He weeps when thinking of intent
from gray unblinking eyes of fish,
alien but not indifferent;
or carpets of eyes on emerald flies,
or the eyes of a beloved milk cow at dawn.
And cool is the night with its thousand eyes,
the night warmed by the breath of owls
with eyes made to feel the objects of dreams.

The day shall come, and the day has come
when all exaltation decays, all
that appears to eyes becomes corrupt.
We move yet blindly, making a world
with a writhing lust to know, to obey,
uncertain of who makes the appeal.

Like Castrati singing with their sweet girl voices
is a world where memory is lost. And we see
through words, and words, and words alone,
which, hovering without their images,
move unencumbered, as disposable as air.
But still, the world turns, and stares.

IX

From airs descend the songs to answer
predicates of latitude
and longitude that measure him.

If his life be a magic square
with the sum of every path the same,
yet the rosined wheel of memory
turns within his awkward soul,
and he sings like a hurdy-gurdy.

Then his rivers of stone and dust
with swirling beauties embodied by blowing
sand sway and wave him past,
reclining behind the perfect mask.

America is a surface land
but thought can descend a thousand feet
to the patient world beneath the street
with age so grand it seems unaged.
Reminders erupt along the paths
that lead him across the bounded state.

No home is ever broad enough
to house his vast expanse of soul.
His home is North America,
and south, and east, and west, and down,
and up – his world is speculative,
and he strings the whole with memory.
There are enough who think him mad,
a dunce, a fool, and shoddily clad.

But none of these does he despise,
nor even those who think him wise.
He rides on Eldorado's wings
and sings and sings and sings and sings:

X

"Round the darkness, round the space,
the theater behind the eyes
is where the sacred finds its place.

On the driftwood hard and dry
the white of passing angels' hair
evokes the wordless parts of mind.

All the rooted memories, bare,
sorted by no motion of will,
bound by cares loose and spare,

instruct the novice, calm, still,
in arts of how minds pry
the heart's braille known by feel.

And like the rise of birds or tides
they do not offer use, but grace
to seize the hidden from inside."

Ray Barfield is an Associate Professor at Duke University in Durham, North Carolina. He has a joint appointment in the Medical School (where he is a pediatric oncologist) and the Divinity School (where he teaches philosophy). His book *The Ancient Quarrel Between Poetry and Philosophy* was recently published by Cambridge University Press. He directs the *Pediatric Quality of Life and Palliative Care Program*, and the Duke initiative called *Theology, Medicine and Culture*.